Good Thinking

– a guide to conscious change –

ISBN 978-1-8383550-9-8

Keekoo Publications

www.keekoo.co.uk

First Edition 2017

Revised Edition 2024

Foreword

This book has been produced to give you some key help for creating positive change in your life. Through developing better, more helpful thoughts, you will improve any situation you find yourself experiencing. It is produced to be dipped into when needed, and comes in two parts – a thought-provoking commentary of desirable activity and simple exercises, followed by 5 quick points of 'best action'.

My sincere hope is that you find something useful in this little book and I wish you well, in whatever choices you make.

Richard

Contents

Introduction and Background

Some might say my early life was pretty secure, coming as I did from a stable background with married parents and two younger siblings. However, by the time I got to 18, my parents had divorced and I was no longer living at home with either of them.

During my life, I have experienced friendships, lovers, marriage, lack of money, and loneliness. I have had several jobs, as well as time unemployed and on benefits. I have also experienced the hardship and stress of being in financial debt. These days, I am self-employed and, whilst by no means rich by conventional standards, pretty much do what I want, when I want, without worry.

I could carry on at some length, about how I got into the mess I did, but this isn't now about me – it's about you.

In this book, I will share with you, the simple things I did, to make changes in my life for the better. This is not one of those books that boasts, 'I was down and out and last year made a million dollars.' We've all been inspired by those stories, only to realise, those people are not us (me). We can certainly aspire to be different from how we are now, but we cannot become someone else.

What you most need now, are some simple methods for changing your circumstances, without it costing you financially.

1. Do you want things to change?

For some, this may seem a ridiculous question. But, it is a question you need to answer before proceeding. If there are advantages to you maintaining your current situation, or being a victim in life, then perhaps you are content to keep things as they are. However, the very fact that this book has come into your possession means that, at some level, you do want to change the life you are experiencing. Answers to questions arrive in many different ways – some of them quite normal; others like suddenly being given this book by a stranger.

If you later decide this book isn't for you, then please pass it on to someone else.

2. The Optimism of Borrowing Money

It took me quite a few years to realise this. But when I was anxious about being able to pay my rent, or pay for repairs on an old car, etc., as soon as I could arrange an increase on my credit cards or consolidate my debt into a new loan, I felt enormous relief. I also felt enormous optimism. 'I'm okay now. I'll be able to get some work to generate some income; I'll try another idea; something will happen; I might even win some money.'

The truth, of course, was that this relief of pressure, leading to a false euphoria, was only transitory. After a few months of managing quite well, treating myself to a few extra gadgets or things for the car or flat, I was back in a similar position, having to 'rob Peter to pay Paul', as they say. Money seemed to slip through my fingers.

In 1984, and needing money for the rent, I decided to look around for things I could sell. I had quite a large collection of old toy cars and train sets, from the 1960s and 70s and they were just starting to grow in value. Also, being of a somewhat 'spiritual' disposition, I didn't want to feel attached to material items. Therefore, I gathered everything up and sent them off to auction. A few weeks later, I received a cheque for about £100. To be honest, it was actually disappointing, because some of the toys were worth more than others and I had expected the auctioneer to sell those separately. Instead, everything was sold as one job lot – over 200 cars and 4 large train sets.

During this time, the UK was experiencing the governance of Margaret Thatcher's Conservative [Tory] Party. By 1984, she was in full swing with her slashing 'reforms' and Yorkshire, where I lived, was in the midst of the 'Miner's Strike' and a lot of heavy-handed, aggressive repression. After this, we had the introduction of a 'Poll Tax' and at the same time, empty buildings became taxable and owners decided it was cheaper to demolish them, than to keep them for future use. Vast areas of Sheffield became much brighter with daylight, as acres of brick rubble – for as far as the eyes could see – took the place of once thriving factories. The Tory party started to sell off a lot of previously nationalised commodities and Ben Elton had started a satirical TV comedy show called, 'Saturday Live' in an attempt to 'wake people up' to what was going on.

I learnt two lessons around this time:

1. If you sell something to raise money to pay the rent for one month, you still need to pay the rent again, the following month. Not only do you have nothing left to sell, but you have sold something that you cannot ever replace.
2. When you consolidate debt, by taking a loan or putting it onto a new credit card, it gives you an opportunity to start building up a new debt, either on the 'now cleared' card or on a new one – thus getting into further debt.

Over a period of about 30 years, my job situation improved and I started to earn better money. However, I had added to my borrowing along the way, and any real benefit through earning more money, was sadly lost through interest repayments. I was still struggling to 'get by' and still carrying the optimism that things would improve. Unfortunately, this optimism was tempered with a growing doubt about my personal self-worth and ability. I started to wonder if it was my lot in life to be poor. Eventually, there wasn't a job I was qualified to do, or that I wanted to do, which would pay me enough to exist in the way I wanted to live. I didn't own my own home and to this day, I have become used to renting. However, I have mostly lived in places that provide a better quality of life, than if I had bought something where I did not want to be.

Throughout these years, I was exploring, shall we say, the more spiritual side of life. There were many questions about my life and existence, which I just couldn't find answers to in conventionally proffered information through religion or science. I read books, attended courses and workshops around the country, and acquired a lot of information on alternative ways to progress through life. However, nothing I tried seemed to bring lasting, positive changes. There would be temporary respite and then a gradual return to the old ways.

One day, it occurred to me that I could really do with a miracle. This led me to thinking about some of the things that had happened in my life and I realised that some of those things were, in a way, miraculous. The only thing was they were not the sort of miraculous things I really wanted.

In 1987, I wrote about my findings in a book called, 'How We Perform Negative Miracles' and 28 years later, I realised that much of what I had written then, not only applied to me now, but I was evidently missing something that I really needed to change my life for the better and with more consistent, longer lasting, positive results.

For the last few years, having more and more, 'walked my talk', life has become much easier and without its previous financial stress. Let me now guide you through some of the things that I have put together, which will help you make a change for the better, in your life.

Some of the items may be a bit alien to your normal way of thinking, and some may be familiar to you – perhaps because you have already tried them or possibly, because you view them as bandwagon, new age thinking, that you normally dismiss – but please read through, and re-read the sections, with as little negative judgement as possible.

3. You Create Your Own Reality

An amazing non-physical entity, known as Seth[1] once said that we all create our own realities. In a

[1] In 1963, Jane Roberts began channelling amazing information from a non-physical entity who called himself Seth. The quality, breadth, and

broad sense, we form our personal beliefs, not only from our own thoughts and experience, but also from that of other people we encounter on our travels through life, whom we resonate with – that is to say, others who seem to feel and respond to life in similar ways to ourselves. As we create our reality, through our thoughts, beliefs, and expectations, we observe it reflected back to us, as physical environment and further experience. This affects us on an emotional level, whereby we want more, or less, of what we are experiencing – and so the process repeats in an on-going fashion.

4. The Physical World as Feedback

Most people separate themselves from the world 'out there' from the world of their private thoughts. We meet physical reality as if it is something already in existence that we encounter, one moment following another. We all have private thoughts and we all form and hold beliefs about our world. However, few people are willing to acknowledge the link between the two. This is further polarised by our modern belief, indeed, faith, in the factual discipline of science: If you cannot measure something, or repeat an experiment to 'prove' something, then its value cannot be measured or validated. The 'not

wisdom of this, became broadly known as The Seth Material and was published in several books. Also visit https://sethcenter.com

understandable' is often then dismissed as unprovable fallacy.

What many fail to appreciate is that science is fixed on its beliefs that we live in a physical universe and therefore can only observe and test anything that is physical – and when I say physical, I mean down to the smallest quantum particles. What science cannot seem to measure, or acknowledge is the non-physical, creative consciousness that is the origin of the physical universe – the origin and ever present something of everything.

In fairness to scientists, some are now willing to accept more of the unexplainable, but mainly in the context of a quantum universe, which produces many of the non-reproducible outcomes that would in the past have been dismissed. Science in this area can demonstrate some very bizarre behaviour. In the early 19th century, Thomas Young's double slit experiment[2] showed that light could be both waves and particles and what occurred depended on whether particles were being observed, or not. These days we talk about quantum entanglement – physicist's acknowledgement that everything is somehow connected. Albert Einstein[3], not a great fan

---

[2] Young's interference experiment - a demonstration that light and matter can display characteristics of both waves and particles

[3] Albert Einstein (1879-1955) – German-born theoretical physicist. Einstein developed the special theory of relativity, one of the two pillars of modern physics.

of quantum physics in his day, described its strange effects as, 'spooky action at a distance'. The closest understandable example might be the difference between someone operating a model plane through an attached wire or, someone doing the same with radio control. In the case of science, it hasn't yet accepted that the radio control connection they cannot understand is what we call, intelligent consciousness. Danish physicist, Niels Bohr[4] once said: "Anyone who is not shocked by quantum theory has not understood it." However, he was still trying to connect his understanding to a physical system, albeit hidden.

5. Law of Attraction

This applies to, and affects, all that exists – not just within the confines of our own physically experienced world, but throughout the whole universe.

To put it simply, wherever you focus your attention, is where energy becomes active. More commonly described as, 'where attention goes, energy flows'.

From a human perspective, we are talking about emotional energy, generated through thought about,

---

[4] Niels Bohr (1885-1962) – Danish physicist who contributed to understanding atomic structure and quantum theory, for which he received the Nobel Prize in Physics in 1922.

or reaction to, something. Through this attention and feeling, you attract towards you, something similar to the emotion you are putting out – whether it is something wanted or unwanted. Strong or accumulated attention, also called focus, will always bring something matching into your experience. When this is coupled with expectation for an outcome, you create changes more rapidly. One of the fastest attractors is fear of something, since most of us find it easier to focus in this area.

Always remember, it is easier to attract things towards you in life, than it is to push them away or repel them.

6. You experience the reality that you create

It is important to start understanding that everything you experience is created by you. A lot of what you think of as reality is a complex illusion; the physical feedback of which is produced to show how well you are using your ability to create outcomes from the action of your creative consciousness.

As you focus your attention with emotion, you gradually affect the way you respond to those thoughts, ideas, and beliefs. This forms a vibrational frequency that emanates from you, electromagnetically, to interface with universal consciousness and form the first building blocks of physical construction. This emanation becomes your principal attractor for all things and events that occur in your life, in your each and every present moment. As you begin to focus your thoughts and feelings differently and with consistency, you can alter this emanation – either for apparent personal benefit or detriment. Ideally, your developing understanding of this fundamental universal principle will help you to attract more beneficial results in your life.

7. Emotions, Beliefs and Expectations

What is emotion? This is the way you feel when you have a personal experience, actual or imagined – that mentally affects you in some way – positively or negatively.

What is a belief? A belief is a thought you keep thinking, until it becomes a truth about something.

What is expectation? Expectation is a strong sense of knowing that something is going to occur.

The combination of emotion + belief + expectation, is very powerful. These are your first building blocks for change.

8. Seeing what is not there

A key ingredient of making a change is to be able to see in the mind, something that you are not seeing through the eyes.

A common mistake most people make is to react to their own creations in a negative way. It's like deliberately breaking a glass and then looking around for someone, or something else, to blame for the cause of the breakage.

Many people in our human societies feel hopeless and powerless to make changes, because they think you have to start from a position of wealth. In actual fact, all you have to do is start with your own ability to think differently. This enables the poorest person on the planet to potentially become the most powerful. Of course, if it was that simple, we'd all be living in a very different world.

9. Arguing for your own limitations

This has become a popular phrase in recent years, but very aptly describes the way many of us defend our reasons for not taking personal responsibility for our actions, denying our ability to handle situations, or our unwillingness to make changes in our lives which could benefit us. I've lost count of the times, in the past, when I would start a sentence with, 'I can't, because...' when in truth, I was either afraid to take part, or simply didn't want to do whatever was on offer, because it did not interest me.

10. Judgement

We live in a world of comparisons; things we like versus things we do not like; what we have and what others have. Through experience, we make decisions and create beliefs about what we consider to be right or wrong, good or bad, or personally valuable. This is fine, so long as we apply our judgement to our own situation, reflecting on our own emotional reaction and asking questions of our own responses. It is not helpful to us, individually or collectively, to make judgements against another, or others. Why? Because in judging others, we are actually judging ourselves. If we are responsible for creating the circumstances and situations reflected back to us in our physical reality, then we have contributed towards the nature of our experience of feeling a need to make such judgements. Let's take a closer look at our role in this creation.

It is rarely a simple matter of obvious feedback, such as dropping a glass and seeing it smash. Our universe is more subtle than that. It is more connected with the on-going emotions that we feel that gradually manifest a physical outcome. Perhaps one of the best examples is to consider health; at its simplest level, mental stress and anxiety, resulting in a physical ailment. Most people can readily identify with that connection, particularly when it results in something obvious, like a headache. What about the same cause with a different outcome – such as a stomach pain, or a skin rash, like psoriasis? Okay, perhaps you can still identify with that. How about your bus not arriving or your car refusing to start? Could it be that a belief about the importance of good time-keeping has caused an underlying anxiety about being late? Could it be that you don't feel like making a particular journey today and need a plausible excuse? The use of illness could help here. If you are unwell, there is no better excuse to avoid doing something. How about being caught up in a 'natural disaster', such as a flood or an earthquake? Now you can begin to see things becoming a bit more complex.

You may not be able to link many of the experiences you have with particular thoughts and feelings, but be assured there will be connections between persistent, underlying, emotional moods, beliefs, and expectations, and the events that you experience throughout your life. You cannot live your life, permanently on guard against 'bad feelings', but what you can do is always reach for the best feelings possible in any situation. You can actually retrain yourself to have a more positive outlook – caring less about, or not taking to heart, things that have usually upset you. For a while, you will continue to have some knee-jerk reactions to situations, but the more you practice having a different feeling, the easier it becomes.

Notice how the more you worry about something, the more prominence it has in your life; how other similar things occur to the ones you think about most. Begin to create new expectations. Let go of as much worry as possible. Just admit: 'There is nothing I can do about this... I trust that the universe knows my situation and will provide something good to help me... even though I do not know what that will be.'

11. Gratitude

Gratitude is a feeling of thankfulness and appreciation. It may seem difficult to feel gratitude at times – particularly when you are experiencing hard times. However, this is another important component you can use to great effect. When you begin to find things to feel good about, more things to feel good about come into your experience.

Start with small things to feel grateful for, such as a cup of tea or coffee, or seeing a flower or feeling physically comfortable in your bed, or sitting in the sun. Look around you and find things you can appreciate. This will become easier and your feelings about your situation will gradually change for the better.

12. Faith and Surrender

When I talk here about faith, I am not linking it to a religious view. Faith simply means you are willing to trust, beyond what may seem to be rational or logical.

Surrender, is a process of letting go. In the practice you are now embarking on, letting go, and not holding onto something, becomes important. Remember, that what you think about is in your head. As Mark Twain once said[5]: "I've had a lot of worries in my life, most of which never happened."

Faith in something you cannot, as yet, experience, is a bit like someone telling you to jump off a cliff and assuring you something will safely catch you. The overwhelming physical evidence is that nothing could be more stupid, than launching yourself into such an obvious, unknown peril. I am not advocating jumping off cliffs, but rather, giving you an analogy of the feeling of what it may be like to buck the trend of mainstream thinking − otherwise known as 'the official line of consciousness', when making a change in the way you decide to do something different. This is the true definition of 'taking a leap of faith'.

---

[5] There is some uncertainty as to the origin of this quote, Mark Twain being the popular choice, but also used by President-elect James A Garfield and others, in slightly different forms.

13. Taking a leap of faith

The problem with most of us though, is that halfway towards the cliff edge, we either step back, or grab hold of a nice, secure rope. We might then fly over the edge, but by continuing to grip our safety rope, we are caught between not being on the firm land and not reaching new ground. We are caught in a limbo of neither one state nor another. Acting on faith can be frightening. This is why most people decide to stay where they are in life and seek more conventional approaches to improving their lot.

Surrender, is the act of letting go – not holding on. The reason it is important to us, is because of how holding on and maintaining attachment can affect our chances of success in creating positive change.

Imagine that you have visualised attracting some more money into your life. You go through a bunch of processes that gets you in the right imaginative frame of mind... and then you keep looking to see if anything is happening. You wonder how your preferred situation is going to manifest itself. You might even decide to give it a helping hand, by buying a lottery ticket. Surely, that will help!

One thing that happens when you really want something is that you feel a heightened lack through not having it. Rather than focusing on the pleasure of having what you want, you focus on the feeling of lack – not having it. This effectively undoes the other work you've done, because now, law of attraction is getting more energy from the feeling of lack, than it is from the feeling of gratitude for having what you want.

When you adopt an attitude of surrender, you basically say: 'This is now out of my control. What will be, will be.' Or to put it another way: 'F**k it!'

The act of surrender is the ultimate leap of faith.

These then – gratitude, faith, and surrender – are your next three building blocks.

14. Letting go

You may think that nothing could be more 'letting go', than the act of surrender. However, the two things are slightly different. Surrender is certainly letting go, but it is letting go with faith that all will work out, with no further input from yourself. The other 'letting go' refers to dropping your attention from whatever it is you have been, up to now, focusing your attention on.

Perhaps the full process might look like this:

• Desiring something with complete attention.
• Imagining and behaving like it already exists.
• Letting go with a nonchalant attitude (seeming not to care).
• Surrendering to whatever outcome might occur, for the benefit of all concerned, with the faith that everything will be just fine.

15. Saying Yes

There's nothing the universe likes more, than someone saying 'yes'. This isn't the 'yes' of, 'okay, if I must do this for you – even though I think you are taking advantage of me.' This is the 'yes' of inspired opportunity. The universe knows what can benefit you; what lines up with the person you really are, the person you can, or want to, become. Learn to 'check in' with yourself. Ask: 'What do I instinctively feel about this?' Go with your first feeling – before the fear, doubt, and excuses take hold.

16. Hard work

Among many cultures and societies, we promote the idea that the harder you work, the more you can achieve or gain. But how do you resolve this when you see some people working in physical labour and still living in poverty, whilst others seem to do very little and receive vast amounts of money? When you reach a point where there is no more time in the day to take on extra work, or you do not have either the qualifications and experience, or the inclination to work harder, or for more hours, then you have to ask yourself, what other options are there? In 2012, I asked myself this same question, which resulted in the conclusion: Conventional work cannot be the only way to receive money.

Following on from this, I decided that the very word, 'work', had all the wrong connotations for me. Work implied toil, sometimes emotional pain, repetitive routine, restriction and limitation. If work was the means to receiving an income, and then you did not work, by definition, you could not 'earn' any money to live. Therefore, I decided: Work has to go!
So what could I replace work with, that would enable me to still receive money?

17. What do you like doing?

As I stared down at a blank sheet of paper, this was my first question. To gain the most from this exercise, you have to be honest with yourself and not fall back into conventional thinking of, 'what could I do to make money?' That was not the question. So what did I like doing?

I enjoyed making things – I liked repairing things and getting them to work again – I'd enjoyed my time working as an audio-visual technician – I liked inventing – I liked playing the piano.

The nagging voice kept completing the sentences: I enjoy making things, but I don't have the space, and the amount of time and effort wouldn't make it viable to make money – I like mending stuff, but I tried that once before, offering to help fix domestic appliances, and I always got given really complicated things, or things that were actually beyond repair or requiring unobtainable new parts – I liked being a technician and enjoyed helping staff and students by ensuring equipment always worked – but it didn't really pay much and with limited promotional opportunities, there was a ceiling on the income that could be achieved – I liked inventing, but that takes time and trying to patent anything is expensive and complicated – I like playing the piano, but I'm not really a musician and my level of ability is amateurish, at best... it's mainly for my own enjoyment.

18. What do you feel like doing?

If you don't get anywhere with the first question of, 'what do I like doing?', then perhaps you have to take a further step back from a conventional approach to 'brainstorming'.

'What I really want to do is hang out with friends, drink coffee, and have interesting conversations.'

'But that's not going to earn you any money!' came the little voice of rational protest.

Be aware, when doing this exercise, of how you are feeling inside when you think about your options. Every time I thought about having to earn money from the things I liked to do, my heart sank, because I also thought about what would be involved to get anything off the ground. But when I imagined having coffee with friends and chatting in a nice relaxed environment, my heart soared. My emotions lifted and I felt lighter.

And then the little voice returned. 'That's nothing to do with earning money.'

With a desire to help others – and something of the natural teacher in me – I set up a Meetup.com group, called 'Chat to Change' and a friend gave me access to a room I could use for free. This gave me both an opportunity to share my experiences and also a context in which to meet new people. One or two people attended each time and I provided free refreshments. The chats were enjoyed by those who attended, but word wasn't spreading and in the end I decided the demand wasn't there and the friendships I'd hoped to make, to carry beyond the sessions, did not materialise, partly, it seemed, because I was seen as teacher and not student, along with the others.

A few weeks later, a friend mentioned a small, informal business group he'd discovered. I went along and soon attended this once a month – getting to know a few more people – drinking tea and coffee together and chatting about the business ideas attendees were trying out. This provided a bit more of a social life and I met many nice people. I made some new contacts – even got a bit of additional website work – but again, did not attract what I would describe as 'developing close friendships', outside of this group's designated meeting times.

On one occasion, a chance comment by our room host led to me teaching art there for a year. I had a wonderful group of people, ranging in age from 30s to 70s, but again, as teacher, I felt almost a moat of separateness between me and the social interaction of the participants. The weekly travel was also becoming a bit tiresome, so in the end, I handed over the group to a former student.

19. Inspired action

The next thing I would like you to practice, is tuning into the thoughts that you have, which are often dismissed as being fleeting, or irrelevant to what you perceive as your current situation. You might call these thoughts 'intuition' or 'flashes of inspiration'; those thoughts that suddenly come from the gut feeling area: 'This doesn't feel right', or 'I'd love to try that.' These are thoughts that you can become aware of, before the 'buts' come to mind.

In the previous section, I shared my experiences of following a desire of having coffee and chatting with friends and although this may not have turned out quite as I had hoped, those experiences resulted from following inspired thoughts, coupled with taking some action in line with those thoughts. The realisation of wanting more, in the way of closer friendships, came after realising a need for something more than just meeting people for coffee and socialising. The important thing I would like you to take from this is the movement from being in one situation, to the transformation into a different situation, that wasn't there previously.

Following inspired action doesn't always lead directly to the goal you end up thinking you wanted to achieve. Inspired action results from the thoughts and feelings you have generated up to the point of the inspired thoughts and ideas coming to your awareness. As another friend once said (and I paraphrase slightly, from memory): "Action tends towards a goal, but when reached, there is a 'dissatisfaction element' which, added to the existing achieved goal, tends towards another desire and new action." This cycle constantly repeats, because we always want new things, new experiences, and new journeys of discovery.

Keep a small notebook

Start to capture these positive fleeting thoughts and write them down. Some of them, you can act on immediately; others you may come back to when the timing feels better. Very often, these little windows of inspiration are calls to action – suggestions from your 'inner knowing self' that are in your best interests to take notice of.

Your inner self is providing feedback, based both on its greater overview of who you really are, together with help, in response to the information you feed it, through your emotional responses to your limited physical experience. You might liken this to someone on the Earth's surface (you), constantly communicating with someone looking at the Earth from outer space (your greater knowing personality) who has unlimited access to information about your personality, the world you experience (and the universe in total) through the most amazing communications network – greater than any internet – and who can 'see' the bigger picture, whilst at the same time, understanding the goals you have pre-set for yourself in this current lifetime experience. This entity is your multidimensional personality – the real you – who can direct you to better places by both arranging appropriate experiences and at the same time communicating suggestions to you through an inner connection – mostly realised as inspired thought and gut feeling.

Because you are often asking, based on discomfort, rather than positive desire, some mixed messages can be sent from you. Your 'cosmic helper' interprets all your thoughts and actions as requests for more similar things. To help with sifting your constantly changing requests, it looks for consistency and repetition, strong desire and powerful expectation. Your only role is to decide where you focus most of your attention. If all of your attention is on debt, your cosmic helper will try to find ways of bringing you more of it. If your focus is on sunny, tropical beaches, your cosmic helper will form ways to bring those conditions closer to being reality in your physical world experience.

If you are providing distorted information about your situation, the cosmic researcher is going to give you suggestions, based on the information you are providing, coupled with its access to other knowledge about you. Your interpretation of all physical feedback events is filtered through your beliefs. You either build on what is in front of you, or you replace it with something built from within you. Done correctly, the evidence of your inner creation will manifest in your physical environment.

If you find yourself feeling stuck and not knowing which way to turn, you might decide to ask your cosmic helper for guidance.

Let's apply this to a hypothetical personal situation. Perhaps you need something specific to get through your day. Your thoughts revolve around: 'How can I get more of what I need? How can I get the money to pay for what I want?' Although afterwards, the 'having' of what you wanted makes you feel better in the short term, you know in your heart that this isn't how you want to live your life. The enormous stress of constantly repeating the process of need and acquisition can be debilitating. Perhaps it is time to ask your cosmic helper some different questions, such as: 'How can I change my situation? How can I come off my dependency for x, y, z, etc? What can I do?

At this point, you must acknowledge the very first thoughts that come to you. Try not to influence the reply. It may not be what you want to hear yourself thinking or saying, but it may hold valuable clues to the best action you can take. If possible, write down your thoughts to read again later.

At first, you may decide to continue as you have done previously, because this change may be too great to bear so suddenly. However, if you keep asking what we might term 'empowering' questions, you will start to shift into a better place. Solutions will begin to show up – many in quite normal ways. Always ask for, and focus on, solutions, rather than thinking about problems. Test out trying the suggestions given in the inspired thoughts that arise immediately after asking your questions. See where you are taken.

20. Probabilities

Probability is a measure of how likely it is that something will occur. In regular physical life, we use past experience, or projected risk assessment, to determine the likely probable outcomes for many situations.

When we talk about personal probabilities, one might say that we draw towards us (law of attraction) the most likely outcomes for events or circumstances that we think about most – both individually and collectively. Repeated experience and an awareness of laws that seem stable in material reality, e.g. gravity, also reside in our psyche as common expectations for certain outcomes. For example, if I drop a china cup on a stone floor, there's a high probability that the cup will break. However, there is also a probable outcome where the cup does not break. The likelihood of a breakage is however, in this example, leaning more in favour of happening than not happening.

Add into this mix, mental focus on such an event occurring in your lifetime and it may not surprise you if, one day, a cup falls off a table and breaks on a floor for you to witness.

If you scale up this process and take a subject that many people in a population may be focusing their attention on, sooner or later an outcome of that focus will present itself in physical feedback – but not necessarily in an immediately obvious way. For example, a concern for our expanding materialism and unfairness in the world might result in a Stock Market crash. Mostly, we share this sort of focus with things that we fear – war, poverty, lack of personal fulfilment. As our collective fear and upset about something grows, it gains momentum. Eventually, it has to manifest in our physical world as an appropriate expression from all the creative conscious focus. It could be anything from a rise in the cost of living to a war somewhere, but it could equally be an earthquake, volcanic eruption, a change in our weather, a change in leadership, or a less obviously connected outcome.

Many of the more noticeable, or larger, events arise out of an inner need among a people, for change of some kind. Often, the precise nature of the change is consciously unknown to the individuals involved, but they just want something different in their experience. The frustration of feeling disempowered to gain something better than their current experience, coupled with not knowing what they can do to bring about a positive change, or even what replacement change is wanted, often spills out as misdirected energy – like a boiling kettle letting off excess steam before it might otherwise explode. It is the eventual lack of containment, for our emotions and expectations, that draws towards us, an experience with its related probabilities and their outcomes – ultimately driving us towards the change we desire, but not necessarily by the means we would have chosen, had we been more conscious in our mental thought processes.

21. What have you got to lose?

Sometimes, one reaches a point where any change is better than no change at all. Unfortunately, we often put ourselves in a mental position of fearing a change, more than we fear the situation we are stuck in and familiar with. Our 'comfort zones' are letting us down. Fear of the unknown is worse than the discomfort of staying where we are.

If you are at a complete loss of what to do, send out a request for assistance to the universe: 'I really don't know what to do to change my situation. Please provide positive guidance that will be easy for me to follow'... or something similar, in your own words. I have used the word 'easy' here, because change does not always have to be hard. You are looking for more ease in your life – not more hardship.

22. The illusion of linear time

In our experience of existing in a physical world, a sense of time allows us to consider our options and firm up our thoughts and ideas. A sense of a past gives us a feeling of evolution and opportunity for reflection; a sense of our present enables us to live in the moment and make conscious changes for our future; and a sense of a future helps us to imagine something that we might like to experience in our next moments of 'now'.

But the actuality of our linear time is that it does not exist. What we have is what Seth[6] calls a "spacious present". From this position, we are able to

---

[6] Op. Cit. Seth – Channelled non-physical personality – Jane Roberts

simultaneously draw on all past and future qualities of our 'multidimensional personality' and bring them together in what he terms "the moment point". However, he also says that a moment point can be an instance or a lifetime of experience. From our previous example of the cosmic helper, think of this connection as private access to your own spacious present – your non-linear time access to all that you require in each moment of your current experience and drive for value fulfilment.[7]

The moment point is our 'now' experience, in conscious realisation. It is the point within which, we can make a change. We can focus our attention on any part of past, present, or future and make of it what we will. It is only within our minds, that we apportion importance. Of course, we are in a constant moment point and therefore, we can choose to make changes constantly, by being aware of what we are thinking and focusing our attention on, moment to moment.

Each thought that you have brings your current experiences and feelings into sharp focus. Each thought builds on another and becomes stronger and 'more solid' with focus and attention.

Have you noticed how thoughts often spiral? How your thinking gains momentum – building emotional

---

[7] Op. Cit. Seth. Value Fulfilment is the driving force of creation

feeling within you? Can you dwell, and build, on happier thoughts, or is it only possible to do this for sad or angry thoughts? Do you feel up-lifted or hopeless after a spell of such deep, inward contemplation?

23. The Spacious Present

Because linear time is an illusion of physical experience, most people do not take advantage of what is available to them in a non-linear way – linear being a series of moments; one following on from the last in a perceived progression from past, to present, to projected future – in the same way we might count 1, 2, 3, 4, rather than 2, 1, 4, 3.

With a spacious present you can, with practice, perceive more holistically – perceiving an overview in the mind, everything that includes you. From this position, you can change the perceived past and future, from your every present moment – what I call your constant moment of 'now'.

Here's an example exercise of being able to change a past event from your present.

1. Think of a past childhood memory that upset you.
2. Think of another childhood memory from the same time period that was happy.

3. Review those experiences from what you know about your life now, but realise that they are memories you hold that no longer exist now, as they did then, in your current, physical experience.

4. Bring forward to the present, the happier of the two memories and for a moment, dwell on the feeling and your emotional response.

5. When you contemplate any past experience, develop an ability of dwelling more on better past memories and less on bad ones. This will change your practised memory of your past for the better and give more brightness in the imagination to the better feeling experiences.

6. Consider too, that people involved or present in a past experience have most likely changed from the way you remember them being, when you were much younger.

Bear in mind, that all of your memories are contained in your mind. In physical terms, they do not actually exist to be experienced in this current moment. What proof, other than your memories of past events, do you have? You might say that other people can corroborate those memories, but consider this: What makes someone else's memory any more accurate or relevant, than your own?

Now of course, there are some events we agree on collectively, either as a group, a culture, or as the human race. But beyond memories and recorded 'history', do these memories – particularly the adverse ones – have to affect you now? And even if you accept some truth about those memories, can you make a new choice as to whether you want them to affect you positively instead of negatively? If you are responding to past memories with a sense of victimhood, can you instead learn something positive and make a decision to promote a better future?

You do not have to go into a state of denial in order to feel better, but you can decide how much you want a thought about something to affect you. What benefit is there for you, to remember something that makes you feel awful? Does your feeling awful help you, or anyone else?

Sometimes, we feel terrible about an experience that hasn't even happened to us. This could be a reflection on a reported historical event, or it could be a contemporary feeling of empathy with someone else's experience. Realise that many experiences are not yours. How much of everyone else's experiences do you want to take on board? How much of the world can you save? How many things can you devote your attention to?

Consider too, that your memory of a past event involving another, or others, may no longer be at the forefront of that person's, or those people's minds. For example, if the event was a situation involving you, that you wish you had handled differently, are you really so important that someone else is going to be thinking about something you said or did, all that time ago, in preference to getting on with their own life, or lives, now?

If you think about it, an individual's memories of events are actually very personal and coloured by the experiences felt at the time, coupled with the beliefs held now. Take for example, Gay Rights. Some cultures have never had a problem with same-sex activity, but many western cultures have held 'moral beliefs' about sexuality only being acceptably expressed in one way. Move forward to the present day, and there is now a different view held and a revised cultural belief that sexuality can be expressed and accepted differently in this area than was previously believed. I am sure attitudes to other sexual practises and gender issues will ultimately change too, as new awareness and understanding removes fears instead of promoting them.

There are many examples, where individual beliefs have been vilified and later accepted by mainstream societies. There will always be people who hold different views. Just because you might become part of an accepted majority, does not automatically mean that you are right – you simple agree at this moment.

Can you split personal belief from moral religious or cultural values? Rules and boundaries are not imposed by an omnipotent consciousness; they are created by humans who want to feel safe in their physical environment. This is reaction to fear-based thinking. When we feel threatened, we want to control. To be able to control, we come together collectively, in agreement, to make rules to impose on everyone – regardless of their part in creating our anxiety. For a while, we feel safer, but it isn't long before we want to make a new rule. This fear-based approach creates more criminals, because each new law spreads a wider net over what is acceptable and further constricts freedom of expression.

Our contemporary society is often based around the notion of competition – survival of the fittest; credited to Darwinism[8], but actually a popularised bastardisation of his theories of evolution in a book by Herbert Spencer.[9] We are nevertheless, encouraged at every opportunity to see this as a positive quality. However, this brings fears of lack and inadequacy for those who cannot compete beyond a certain perceived level, or wish to do so. Instead of co-operation, it promotes selfishness. If our society was set up around ideas of co-operation and wanting the best for everyone, we would always want to support the success of others – knowing that we can all benefit by helping one another to be the best we can become. Most people innately like to

---

[8] Charles Robert Darwin (1809-1882) was an English naturalist, best known for his contributions to the science of evolution.

[9] Herbert Spencer (1820-1903) was an English philosopher, biologist, anthropologist, sociologist, and also a prominent classical liberal political theorist, who coined the term 'survival of the fittest' in his 1864 book, 'Principles of Biology'.

help; we feel good when someone has appreciated a kind act – it's uplifting.

Consider that whatever you are thinking most strongly about, now, is what you are projecting forward. The best way to see your future is to imagine living the experiences you want to be having in your 'now' moment. This takes practice because you have to ignore patterns of resistance and the life you are witnessing around you. Realise that, in a way, what you perceive around you is more past than present; it is what you have created up to this moment. To change your physical experience, you have to change how you see your experience inside your mind's eye. If there are already some good things in your present experience, build on those. If there are experiences you do not like, don't push against them; simply accept their presence and imagine either favourable resolutions, or alternative experiences, in their place.

Learn to daydream more often

Many of us are familiar with school teachers saying in classrooms: 'Stop daydreaming and pay attention!' The odd thing is that this is often a shared opinion that didn't directly happen to most of those who share it. However, it would have been better in those instances where it did happen, if teachers had run guided daydreaming sessions. The process of creative change begins in our minds.

24. Acceptance without Judgement

This is not easy for most people to master. We all make judgements, either based on comparisons of like or don't like, or based on moral views – that's right or wrong. Either way, it comes down to our beliefs about the experience we have involved ourselves in.

Let's consider the judgement of another person. Here are some thoughts we might have:

1. I wouldn't do that – so he/she shouldn't be allowed to.
2. That is morally or ethically wrong.
3. I wish I could do that, but I can't.
4. An eye for an eye. He/she must be punished. (False understanding of Karma[10]).
5. Minding someone else's business.

Here are some rationales behind the above thoughts:

1. I take the self-righteous position because I personally find it easy to act or respond in a different [right] way.
2. Whose morals and ethics? Who decides what is right or wrong, and why?
3. Jealousy, coupled with a fear of being caught by someone.
4. Retribution for an action that has upset you

---

[10] Karma – the eastern tradition of cause and effect; of retribution and balance, for personal or collective actions.

5. Self-appointed policing of another or others.

Why is it not helpful to judge other people?

Everyone on our physical planet is doing the best they can with what they have available, both in terms of knowledge and resources. We all want to experience happiness and fulfilment. We are all creating from our own understanding. We cannot all be the same and when we feel forced into any type of conformity, many of us rebel.

Biblically speaking, one might borrow the phrase: 'Let he who has not sinned, cast the first stone'. In other words, no one is perfect, in this context, and we have all done things that we may have regretted. However, most of us eventually learn by our actions, things that we will handle differently next time. What is important to also realise, is that someone else may need a personal experience before he or she can gain a similar understanding to ours. Conversely, their understanding could equally be quite different, but no less valuable. In terms of making judgements, we must also consider that our conclusion about someone or something could be wrong. We can easily misinterpret, due to our own belief filters and biases. A good simple example of this would be someone who cannot find their wallet and immediately blames someone else for stealing it. A few minutes later, it turns up under a pile of clothes.

Of course, as our populations have expanded, collectives have formed to try and create stability through control. Laws are passed and punishments are used to enforce them. As more people discover new ways to 'upset' other people, more laws are created and more of us become criminalised, as a result. We appoint people, specifically to make judgements on others and we stir up outrage through public media channels, to vindicate our positions of righteousness. We think that by controlling people to behave and do things the way we would do them, the world will be a better and safer place.

We are told that no one ever succeeds without making some mistakes along the way, but in the same breath, we are also told that people cannot afford to make mistakes. And when someone of adult age makes a mistake, they must be punished appropriately, because we have to apportion appropriate blame, to make ourselves feel better.

Once you accept the notion that people are different and have different ways of behaving, including yourself, then you can let go of the angst – or at least you can allow yourself only a brief upset, before moving on.

Let's see if we can expand our understanding on the subject of judgement and find ways of changing the way we respond to it.

25. Ho'oponopono

Ho'oponopono (ho-o-pono-pono) is an ancient Hawaiian practice of reconciliation and forgiveness which literally means, to 'make right'. It is also referred to as 'SITH' (Self Identity Through Ho'oponopono) by its originator in this form, Morrnah N Simeona[11] and subsequently taught by former clinical psychologist, Dr Ihaleakala Hew Len (who had successfully used the 'cleaning' techniques in a Hawaiian State Hospital for mentally ill criminals).

I first came across Ho'oponopono via a friend. As it wasn't something that immediately grabbed my interest at the time, I passed the information on to another friend who I thought might be interested. She in turn decided to travel to Hawaii to discover more, and attended a course with Dr Hew Len. After seeing how using Ho'oponopono rapidly changed some difficult circumstances in my friend's life, I decided to take another look at it myself. To my surprise, it seemed to improve any situation I directed my attention towards, whilst reciting a simple mantra.[12] I have introduced Ho'oponopono to other friends and without exception everyone has reported positive changes in their lives, as well as

---

[11] Morrnah N Simeona (1913–1992) – was a native Hawaiian Kahuna (in Hawaii, a wise man or shaman) and gifted healer.

[12] A mantra is a commonly repeated word or phrase.

benefits for people and situations included in their thoughts, whilst reciting the basic mantra.

The basic premise of Ho'oponopono is linked to this question that Dr Hew Len says we must ask ourselves when faced with any situation or circumstance that we would rather change:

**What is it within me,
that is attracting this situation?**

The power of this question resides in each individual accepting full responsibility for everything that comes into his or her personal life awareness. For example, Dr Hew Len realised that for mentally ill criminals to show up in his life, he had to be, at some level, creating them. (Remember our responsibility for creating our own realities). By 'cleaning' on and healing his own thoughts and feelings, he gradually saw those same people leaving his experience – very often by recovering or sometimes being transferred to other accommodation, until eventually, the Hospital was closed. (This example also relates to what I mentioned earlier about many things in our world being opposite to what we think they are. Often in our physical experience, it is the [feedback] symptom we see and react to – not the cause).

Seth, and also Abraham,[13] informs us that every individual creates his or her own reality and is fully responsible for doing so. Once you accept this, the Hew Len question makes more sense. It links directly to the law of attraction, personal beliefs, and expectations.

How and why, do we create our own reality?

How? By projecting our thoughts and beliefs electromagnetically, to interface with the atomic level physical building blocks, we form our physical world.

Why? As a self-actualised entity, of the universal intelligent consciousness that creates all things, we want to be a participant in our own observations, acquisition of knowledge, and understanding. We practice manipulating energy through creative, mental focus, resulting in the production of new physical things, relationships, and environments, so that we can eventually master what is sometimes referred to as, conscious creation.

Why is it good to accept 100% responsibility?

When you accept that you are fully responsible for creating everything that happens in your life, you stop blaming others and you stop arguing for your

---

[13] Abraham is a collective of non-physical teachers, "interpreted" by Esther Hicks.

own limitations. It's actually very empowering, because if you are the one creating your life – and perhaps it feels at times, terrible – then you are the one who can change your life.

How do I change my life?

Having accepted personal responsibility, the next thing is to envision your life the way you would like it to be, as if you are already experiencing what you desire. At first, you may feel this is not easy, since you are in the practice of automatically continuing the vision of your life from the currently accepted position – whatever that may be. But remember something else: what you see around you, is what you have already created. In order to change what you see, for something different, you must first imagine inside yourself, something different, regardless of what appears to be present in physical reality around you. When you can envision a change with clarity, coupled with a feeling of expectation that change has happened, the universe has to adjust your next physical experience to match your vision.

So what's the catch?

Not so much a catch, as a problem of being able to focus your attention. Furthermore, this process of change often requires something more – a leap of faith – that you begin responding to the new beliefs you are creating, even though they are not yet showing up. Here is your first life-changing tool:

Ho'oponopono mantra

This is your 'cleaning' tool. Simply recite the following mantra, constantly, whilst allowing any thoughts to enter your mind.

For example, if you can't stop thinking about a debt, an argument, or some other upset, simply let the associated thoughts come to mind and keep saying the mantra, inside your head – or out loud, if you want to:

I'm sorry
Please forgive me
I love you
Thank you

No explanation of why this is so effective is necessary to understand, for it to work, but if you want to know more, just look it up online. Simply repeat the mantra over and over, whilst holding any thought in your mind that you want to cleanse. Once you start, you will probably find that more thoughts and their associated feelings will surface for cleaning. Just keep going until it feels comfortable to stop. Use the mantra as often as you like. The main thing is to remember to use it. Don't treat it like a sandwich toaster – using it every day for a week, putting it away in the cupboard and suddenly rediscovering it a year later!

What is the significance of the words?

I'm sorry: Apologising for creating this situation in my life.

Please forgive me: I ask myself and the situation for forgiveness.

I love you: This performs the dual role of affirming that I love whatever is affecting me and I also love myself.

Thank you: Giving thanks for the expected improved outcome.

26. Focus for 68 seconds

Your next tool is used to help you focus your attention, long enough to kick in the law of attraction process. It was originally described by Abraham.[14] The premise was that we all put too much effort into trying to change things through excessive physical effort, when all we really have to do, is focus our emotional thought energy for a short time. Abraham tells us that the process of law of attraction starts after only 17 seconds of focused thought and is

---

[14] Op. Cit. Abraham and Esther Hicks

equivalent to 2,000 action hours of physical effort. By the time we get to 68 seconds, we are apparently up to 2 million action hours.

I suggest you use a stopwatch at first, and write down your thoughts on paper. If you lose concentration before the 68 seconds is up, start again from scratch. Writing your thoughts down, at least when you begin this practice, helps to further focus your attention, stops your mind from drifting, and makes you think about what you are wishing to attract. You can also review what you have written, without trying to remember what you were otherwise imagining in your head.

27. Resistance stops receipt

Imagine a tug-of-war, where two opposing teams of equally matched individuals attempt to pull a rope marker across a line. This is how most people are with their visualisations. You want something... but then immediately start thinking of why you can't have it.

This is what occurs when you develop your abilities with law of attraction. The message we often send out in our vibration is: I want it, but I don't. I'd like it, but I can't have it because...

You might say that you don't do that, but you still don't get the things you desire. One reason for this is 'root assumptions' or 'root beliefs'. Regardless of what you think about in this moment of 'now', you might have spent quite a while in your life, believing that some things cannot happen, either because you have been told they cannot happen factually or scientifically, or because somewhere, you have convinced yourself of their unlikeliness or impossibility – in your experience. So although you desire a change in your life, and are not consciously reflecting on the plausibility, something resides within your being that has a stronger, opposing belief, than the one you are now focusing on. Therefore, your general vibration and frequency of output is of a fairly consistent nature, regardless of your inspired highs or desperate lows. What you are aiming for is a new consistency. You could call it your modus operandi or your normal knee-jerk reaction to events.

For example, your first reaction to any upsetting situation might be, 'It's a disaster!' – followed by all the associated emotion and physical actions. With a more mindful awareness you may gradually change this and when you notice that your first reaction is more like, 'that's okay – no need to give energy to this.' – And you don't feel the need to physically respond with outrage – then you know you have successfully changed.

There are a few things you can try out to develop this:

• Write down something you want.
• Write down the reasons you want this.
• Write down the reasons you believe you will have this.
• Write down anything that might make this difficult.
• Write down any belief you have about any aspect of your desire and whether this belief holds any truth. Seek the origin of the belief. Form a new, more helpful, belief to put in its place and then actively look for evidence of your new belief – as you have always done with your old one!
• Repeat the first 3 again.

28. Request assistance

Sometimes it is difficult to know what to do, how to change something, or even know what to ask. Before you go to sleep, send out the thought: I would like to gain clarity about... [add here the thing you want clarity about]. Try to keep your request simple. You may need to repeat your request over the course of a few nights.

Here are a few examples:

• I want clarity about what I want.

- I want help with my ability to focus my thoughts in more positive ways.
- I want help to attract more money.
- I want help with getting a place to live.
- I want help to attract a lover or partner.
- I want help to feel better.
- I want help with improving my health.

The request can be about anything, but keep it as clear as you can. You can repeat the same request as often as you like. You do not have to look for the answer. You will probably find that some new clarity just comes to you and it could be via any number of ways.

One thing I have noticed is that the universe will often deliver answers in ways that seem quite ordinary. A friend may send you a link to a website, or pass on a book to you that has the very information you have been asking about. You might overhear a conversation or see something written on a bill board. You might be walking and suddenly a dog barks which triggers an idea in your mind. All these things seem quite ordinary and quite removed from the bearded guru you were expecting to see materialize in front of you, with the answer to all your problems.

I remember when I first noticed this ordinary feedback. I had reached a point where I felt I had all the information I now needed to progress my spiritual evolution. I wasn't particularly interested in other people recommending books and videos to me on subjects I already knew enough about, or that might detract from the focus I wanted to maintain. Sometimes I felt my ego prodding me with its annoyance. But gradually it dawned on me that by accepting some of these recommendations, I was allowing the universe to give me a bit more information that I had been thinking about – something to increase my clarity and understanding.

Sometimes, you are the channel for someone else's clarity. The universe will use whatever means it has at its disposal – and usually takes the quickest and easiest route.

29. Taking the path of least resistance

Most of us have grown up with the belief that we must work hard to achieve anything. Spiritual philosophies, on the other hand, have often extolled the virtue of least resistance; going with the flow; relaxing and letting the current take you where it will. The contemporary spiritual view is that hard work symbolises inner resistance. When something is going well, it is flowing with ease. The notion that pushing against something harder, will move it, is not one that we should be encouraging for every activity we are involved with. At such times when we do apply physical effort, it should feel joyful and exhilarating.

30. Understanding deliberate creation

Every time you have a thought about something, there is a 'probable outcome' associated with that thought. Depending on your focus, some probabilities become more likely to manifest than others – but all exist together. Remember the well-known saying, where attention goes, energy flows.

Let me share a bit of general advice:

• Consciously feel good about as many things as you can – every day.
• Ask aloud: 'How can it get any better than this? What else is possible?'
• Get into a habit of thinking about best-case scenarios.
• Focus on solutions rather than problems.
• Avoid watching negative current affairs, emotionally charged news, soaps, and negatively biased 'reality TV' shows.
• Be mindful of your self-talk[15] and the things you say in conversation with others.

---

[15] Self-talk is what you say to yourself, either through inner dialogue or expressed audibly.

• If you hear yourself saying something out of habit, ask yourself if it is really true for you – perhaps you want to change that old belief.

• Be mindful of the judgements you make in relation to others – you're only judging yourself.

• Emotional feelings that you have are your inner guidance system – act on them.

• Keep a little notebook and write down any inspired thoughts you don't want to act on immediately – and periodically look through it.

• Realise that physical reality is only personal feedback for you – if you want to know what your vibrational output is like, simply observe what is around you in your daily life.

• Offer gratitude as often as you can and thank whatever feedback comes your way

• Desire with emotion and positive expectation, but with no attachment to outcome.

• Develop the feeling of knowing that everything will turn out for the best and highest good of everyone – including you.

• Accept that everyone is doing their best with whatever they have access to.

• Nothing is so important that you need to be anxious about it – imagine looking at the Earth from space, before zooming back in on the little bit of physical stuff that is your experience.

• Get yourself an 'Easy button' [originally from Staples] – press it every time something positive happens with little effort on your part and listen to it say, "That was easy!"

- If the only time you can make a difference is in every moment of 'now', actively decide on as many desirable things as possible.
- Start writing down positive things about your new life as if they exist now. It's a great way to focus your attention long enough to let law of attraction kick in – which according to Abraham[16] starts at only 17 seconds.
- The universe is a safe place if you allow it to be. Experiment with trusting the universe.
- Always intend to do what you enjoy most
- Pay attention to how you feel – not just in the moment, but over a period of time.

31. Analogies of progression

When you start living your life with different thoughts and a different perspective, you may feel for a while, that nothing much is changing. The first part of trust is to stop sitting on the fence, trying to decide which side has the greener grass or the safest path.

Your first 'different feeling' will probably occur a little while after you have jumped off the fence. You know that you have made a decision, but you can still see the fence and it is close enough to climb back onto in your moments of doubt.

---

[16] Op. Cit. Abraham

If you stick to your resolve and continue to explore your new beliefs about your life, the next feeling you may have is turning around and noticing that the fence is a long way from where you thought you were standing... and you feel a bit odd.

And then, one day, you will suddenly feel a bit like this:

It's a feeling that generally defies expression or description, since it is one of those that you can only know personally, once you have experienced it – sometimes called a 'quale'[17] experience.

32. The Panic Reaction

---

[17] (Philosophy) an ineffable conscious experience, as distinct from any physical or computational process

You find yourself in a situation that starts to produce feelings of stress. Your automatic responses start to surface – kicking in just as they always used to. There is however, this time, a conscious thought of not wanting to react in this way. You've done all the mental work, recited your Ho'oponopono, accepted responsibility for creating your experiences – and yet, you are once again frustrated by circumstances that seem to be coming at you from 'out there'! It can be so hard to have a different thought; to refocus your attention in more positive and helpful ways.

But you must persevere. Each time you have this type of experience and each time you ask yourself, "What is it within me that is attracting this situation?" you ease the pressure, reducing the strength of the energy associated with it. You may not be able to answer the question immediately, but with a bit of inner searching, reasons for attracting the experience may come to the surface.

The fastest way to put out the fire is to starve it of fuel and oxygen. Try not to respond for a moment. Take a breath or turn away... even leave the location for a while.

Those who live life by default will doubtless find it easy to link one negative thought to another. If only we could do that as easily as when thinking of wonderful things we would like to happen.

Remember the 17 second accumulation, mentioned earlier, works for negative as well as positive thoughts. Whatever you feed with your thoughts and energy continues to exist and expand.

The feedback you receive from the physical environment is always a perfect reflection of the vibration you have been emanating, but in your terms of understanding, it often appears to manifest differently to its cause – sometimes making it difficult to see the connection. For example, missing your bus, or not being able to start your car, could be a way for the universe to grant your wish to avoid doing something that would demand an acceptable excuse not to participate. Often we do not make the full connection. Instead we curse our bad luck at missing the bus or our car not working, but forget that we didn't feel like doing something we simultaneously felt we had to do!

33. A quote from Seth

"Experience is the product of the mind, the spirit, conscious thoughts and feelings, and unconscious thoughts and feelings. These together form the reality that you know. You are hardly at the mercy of a reality, therefore, that exists apart from yourself, or is thrust upon you.

"You are so intimately connected with the physical events composing your life experience that often you

cannot distinguish between the seemingly material occurrences and the thoughts, expectations and desires that gave them birth. If there are strongly negative characteristics present in your most intimate thoughts, if these actually form bars between you and a more full life, still you often look through the bars, not seeing them. Until they are recognized they are impediments.

"Even obstacles have a reason for being. If they are your own, then it is up to you to recognize them and discover the circumstances behind their existence.

"Your conscious thoughts can be great clues in uncovering such obstructions. You are not nearly as familiar with your own thoughts as you may imagine. They can escape from you like water through your fingers, carrying with them vital nutrients that spread across the landscape of your psyche—and all too often carrying sludge and mud that clog up the channels of experience and creativity...

"What exists physically exists first in thought and feeling. There is no other rule. ... As soon as you recognize this fact, you can begin at once to alter those conditions that cause you dismay or dissatisfaction."[18]

---

[18] The Nature of Personal Reality, Preface, Session 609

A quick guide to changing any situation

Acknowledge the situation

Recognise that you have responded in a way that you want to change.

Ask the question

What is it within me, that is creating this situation?

Clean on it

Repeatedly recite the Ho'oponopono mantra:

I'm sorry
Please forgive me
I love you
Thank you

Focus on the solution

Imagine, with positive expectation, having the outcome you would like to have, as if it exists now.

Relax

Let go. Stop thinking about it. The universe has got your message.

www.ingramcontent.com/pod-product-compliance
Lightning Source LLC
Chambersburg PA
CBHW032029040426
42448CB00006B/782